Farrukh Arslan

Current trends in Computer Systems

Farrukh Arslan

Current trends in Computer Systems

LAP LAMBERT Academic Publishing

Imprint
Any brand names and product names mentioned in this book are subject to
trademark, brand or patent protection and are trademarks or registered
trademarks of their respective holders. The use of brand names, product
names, common names, trade names, product descriptions etc. even without
a particular marking in this work is in no way to be construed to mean that
such names may be regarded as unrestricted in respect of trademark and
brand protection legislation and could thus be used by anyone.

Cover image: www.ingimage.com

Publisher:
LAP LAMBERT Academic Publishing
is a trademark of
International Book Market Service Ltd., member of OmniScriptum Publishing
Group
17 Meldrum Street, Beau Bassin 71504, Mauritius
Printed at: see last page
ISBN: 978-620-3-58164-5

Current Trends in Computer Systems

By

FARRUKH ARSLAN, Ph.D.

TABLE OF CONTENTS

LIST OF TABLES

LIST OF FIGURES

1   **INTRODUCTION**   **5**

    1.1 How a Computer Works

    1.2 Input: Getting Data from the User to the Computer

    1.3 Source Data Automation: Collecting Data Where It Starts

    1.4 Output: Information for the User

    1.5 Computer Graphics

2   **MASSIVE MULTIPLAYER ONLINE GAMES**   **23**

    2.1 Service oriented architecture

    2.2 SOA for MMOG

    2.3 Simulation of SOA concept for servers

    2.4 Simulation flow in BPEL

    2.5 Middle-ware for MMOG

    2.6 MMOG requirements and solutions

3   **SOFTWARE SYSTEMS AND COST ESTIMATION**   **34**

    3.1 Machine Learning Algorithms

    3.2 Datasets and Evaluation Criteria

    3.3 Data Mining

4   **COMPUTER NETWORKS AND COMMUNICATION SYSTEMS**   **46**

    4.1 Problem Formulation

    4.2 Rate of Convergence

    4.3 Ensemble-Averaged Square Error

    4.4 Computational Complexity

5   **Future Work**   **52**

BIBLIOGRAPHY   **53**

LIST OF TABLES

Table

1   An SQL based database holds the user attributes

2   Comparing DDS with other Technologies

3   Datasets attributes description

4   Performance results on dataset 1

5   Performance results on dataset 2

6   Performance results on dataset 3

LIST OF FIGURES

Figure

1.   Mean Square Error (MSE) methodology

2   Convergence of LMS technique

1. INTRODUCTION

This chapter is a brief summary of the history of Computers. The first substantial computer was the giant ENIAC machine by John W. Mauchly and J. Presper Eckert at the University of Pennsylvania. ENIAC (Electrical Numerical Integrator and Calculator) used a word of 10 decimal digits instead of binary ones like previous automated calculators/computers. ENIAC was also the first machine to use more than 2,000 vacuum tubes, using nearly 18,000 vacuum tubes. Storage of all those vacuum tubes and the machinery required to keep the cool took up over 167 square meters (1800 square feet) of floor space. Nonetheless, it had punched-card input and output and arithmetically had 1 multiplier, 1 divider-square rooter, and 20 adders employing decimal "ring counters," which served as adders and also as quick-access (0.0002 seconds) read-write register storage.

The executable instructions composing a program were embodied in the separate units of ENIAC, which were plugged together to form a route through the machine for the flow of computations. These connections had to be redone for each different problem, together with presetting function tables and switches. This "wire-your-own" instruction technique was inconvenient, and only with some license could ENIAC be considered programmable; it was, however, efficient in handling the particular programs for which it had been designed. ENIAC is generally acknowledged to be the first successful high-speed electronic digital computer (EDC) and was productively used from 1946 to 1955. A controversy developed in 1971, however, over the patentability of ENIAC's basic digital concepts, the claim being made that another U.S. physicist, John V. Atanasoff, had already used the same ideas in a simpler vacuum-tube device he built in the 1930s while at Iowa State College. In 1973, the court found in favor of the company using Atanasoff's claim and Atanasoff received the acclaim he rightly deserved.

The 1960s saw large mainframe computers become much more common in large industries and with the US military and space program. IBM became the unquestioned market leader in selling these large, expensive, error-prone, and very hard to use machines.

A veritable explosion of personal computers occurred in the early 1970s, starting with Steve Jobs and Steve Wozniak exhibiting the first Apple II at the First West Coast Computer Faire in San Francisco. The Apple II boasted a built-in BASIC programming language, color graphics, and a 4100 character memory for only $1298. Programs and data could be stored on an everyday audio-cassette recorder. Before the end of the fair, Wozniak and Jobs had secured 300 orders for the Apple II and from there Apple just took off.

Also introduced in 1977 was the TRS-80. This was a home computer manufactured by Tandy Radio Shack. In its second incarnation, the TRS-80 Model II, came complete with a 64,000 character memory and a disk drive to store programs and data on. At this time, only Apple and TRS had machines with disk drives. With the introduction of the disk drive, personal computer applications took off as a floppy disk was a most convenient publishing medium for distribution of software.

IBM, which up to this time had been producing mainframes and minicomputers for medium to large-sized businesses, decided that it had to get into the act and started working on the Acorn, which would later be called the IBM PC. The PC was the first computer designed for the home market which would feature modular design so that pieces could easily be added to the architecture. Most of the components, surprisingly, came from outside of IBM, since building it with IBM parts would have cost too much for the home computer market. When it was introduced, the PC came with a 16,000 character memory, keyboard from an IBM electric typewriter, and a connection for tape cassette player for $1265.

By 1984, Apple and IBM had come out with new models. Apple released the first generation Macintosh, which was the first computer to come with a graphical user interface(GUI) and a mouse. The GUI made the machine much more attractive to home computer users because it was easy to use. Sales of the Macintosh soared like nothing ever seen before. IBM was hot on Apple's tail and released the 286-AT, which with applications like Lotus 1-2-3, a spreadsheet, and Microsoft Word, quickly became the favourite of business concerns.

That brings us up to about ten years ago. Now people have their own personal graphics workstations and powerful home computers. The average computer a person might have in their home is more powerful by several orders of magnitude than a machine like ENIAC. The computer revolution has been the fastest growing technology in man's history.

1.1 How a Computer Works

The central processing unit is the unseen part of a computer system, and users are only dimly aware of it. But users are very much aware of the input and output associated with the computer. They submit input data to the computer to get processed information, the output.

Sometimes the output is an instant reaction to the input. Consider these examples:
Zebra-striped bar codes on supermarket items provide input that permits instant retrieval of outputs - price and item name - right at the checkout counter.
A bank teller queries the computer through the small terminal at the window by giving a customer's account number as input. The same screen immediately provides the customer's account balance as output.
A forklift operator speaks directly to a computer through a microphone. Words like left, right, and lift are the actual input data. The output is the computer's instant response, which causes the forklift to operate as requested.
A medical student studies the human body on a computer screen, inputting changes to the program to show a close-up of the leg and then to remove layers of tissue to reveal the muscles and bone underneath. The screen outputs the changes, allowing the student (without donning a mask, sanitary gloves, or operating gown) to simulate surgery on the computer.
A sales representative uses an instrument that looks like a pen to enter an order on a special pad. The handwritten characters are displayed as "typed" text and are stored in the pad, which is actually a small computer.

Input and output may sometimes be separated by time or distance or both. Here are some examples:

Factory workers input data by punching in on a time clock as they go from task to task. The time clock is connected to a computer. The outputs are their weekly paychecks and reports for management that summarize hours per project on a quarterly basis.

A college student writes checks. The data on the checks is used as input to the bank computer, which eventually processes the data to prepare a bank statement once a month.

Charge-card transactions in a retail store provide input data that is processed monthly to produce customer bills.

Water-sample data is collected at lake and river sites, keyed in at the environmental agency office, and used to produce reports that show patterns of water quality.

The examples in this section show the diversity of computer applications, but in all cases the process is the same: input-processing-output. We have already had an introduction to processing. Now, in this section we will examine input and output methods in detail.

1.2   Input: Getting Data from the User to the Computer

Some input data can go directly to the computer for processing. Input in this category includes bar codes, speech that enters the computer through a microphone, and data entered by means of a device that converts motions to on-screen action. Some input data, however, goes through a good deal of intermediate handling, such as when it is copied from a source document and translated to a medium that a machine can read, such as a magnetic disk. In either case the task is to gather data to be processed by the computer 唱ometimes called raw data and convert it into some form the computer can understand.

Keyboard

A keyboard is usually part of a personal computer or part of a terminal that is connected to a computer somewhere else. Not all keyboards are traditional, however. A fast-food franchise like McDonald's, for example, uses keyboards whose keys represent items such as large fries or a Big Mac. Even less traditional in the United States are keyboards that are used to enter Chinese characters.

Mouse

A mouse is an input device with a ball on its underside that is rolled on a flat surface, usually the desk on which the computer sits. The rolling movement causes a corresponding movement on the screen. Moving the mouse allows you to reposition the pointer, or cursor, an indicator on the screen that shows where the next interaction with the computer can take place. The cursor can also be moved by pressing various keyboard keys. You can communicate commands to the computer by pressing a button on top of the mouse. In particular, a mouse button is often used to click on an icon, a pictorial symbol on a screen; the icon represents a computer activity-a command to the computer-so clicking the icon invokes the command.

Trackball

A variation on the mouse is the trackball. You may have used a trackball to play a video game. The trackball is like an upside-down mouse-you roll the ball directly with your hand. The popularity of the trackball surged with the advent of laptop computers, when traveling users found themselves without a flat surface on which to roll the traditional mouse.

1.3   Source Data Automation: Collecting Data Where It Starts

Efficient data input means reducing the number of intermediate steps required between the origination of data and its processing. This is best accomplished by source data automation use of special equipment to collect data at the source, as a by-product of the activity that generates the data, and send it directly to the computer. Recall, for example, the supermarket bar code, which can be used to send data about the product directly to the computer. Source data automation eliminates keying, thereby reducing costs and opportunities for human-introduced mistakes. Since data about a transaction is collected when and where the transaction takes place, source data automation also improves the speed of the input operation.

For convenience, we will divide this discussion into the primary areas related to source data automation: magnetic-ink character recognition, optical recognition, data collection devices, and even directly by your own voice, finger, or eye. Let us consider each of these in turn.

Magnetic-Ink Character Recognition

Abbreviated MICR, magnetic-ink character recognition is a method of machine-reading characters made of magnetized particles. The most common example of magnetic characters is the array of numbers across the bottom of your personal check.

Most magnetic-ink characters are preprinted on your check. If you compare a check you wrote that has been cashed and cleared by the bank with those that are still unused in your checkbook, you will note that the amount of the cashed check has been reproduced in magnetic characters in the lower-right corner. These characters were added by a person at the bank by using a MICR inscriber.

An inexpensive way to get entire documents, pictures, and anything on a flat Surface into a computer is by using a scanner. Scanners use optical recognition systems that have a light beam to scan input data to convert it into electrical signals, which are sent to the computer for processing. Optical recognition is by far the most common type of source input, appearing in a variety of ways: optical marks, optical characters, bar codes, handwritten characters, and images. Scanners use Optical Character Recognition software, described below, to translate text on scanned documents into text that is suitable for word processors and other computer applications.

Optical Mark Recognition

Abbreviated OMR, optical mark recognition is sometimes called mark sensing, because a machine senses marks on a piece of paper. As a student, you may immediately recognize this approach as the technique used to score certain tests. Using a pencil, you make a mark in a specified box or space that corresponds to what you think is the answer. The answer sheet is then graded by a device that uses a light beam to recognize the marks and convert them to computer-recognizable electrical signals.

Optical Character Recognition

Abbreviated OCR, optical character recognition devices also use a light source to read special characters and convert them into electrical signals to be sent to the central processing unit. The characters-letters, numbers, and special symbols-can be read by both humans and machines.

They are often found on sales tags on store merchandise. A standard typeface for optical characters, called OCR-A, has been established by the American National Standards Institute.

The handheld wand reader is a popular input device for reading OCR-A. There is an increasing use of wands in libraries, hospitals, and factories, as well as in retail stores. In retail stores the wand reader is connected to a point-of-sale (POS) terminal. This terminal is somewhat like a cash register, but it performs many more functions. When a clerk passes the wand reader over the price tag, the computer uses the input merchandise number to retrieve a description (and possibly the price, if not on the tag) of the item. A small printer produces a customer receipt that shows the item description and price. The computer calculates the subtotal, the sales tax (if any), and the total. This information is displayed on the screen and printed on the receipt; notice that both screen and printer are output, so the POS terminal is a complex machine that performs both input and output functions. Finally, some POS terminals include a device that will accept a credit card, inputting account data from the magnetic strip on a customer's charge card.

The raw purchase data becomes valuable information when it is summarized by the computer system. This information can be used by the accounting department to keep track of how much money is taken in each day, by buyers to determine what merchandise should be reordered, and by the marketing department to analyze the effectiveness of their ad campaigns.

Bar Codes
Each product on the store shelf has its own unique number, which is part of the Universal Product Code (UPC). This code number is represented on the product label by a pattern of vertical marks, or bars, called bar codes. (UPC, by the way, is an agreed-upon standard within the supermarket industry; other kinds of bar codes exist. You need only look as far as the back cover of this book to see an example of another kind of bar code.) These zebra stripes can be sensed and read by a bar code reader, a photo- electric device that reads the code by means of reflected light. As with the wand reader in a retail store, the bar code reader in a bookstore or grocery store is part of a point-of-sale terminal. When you buy, say, a can of corn at the supermarket, the checker moves it past the bar code reader. The bar code merely identifies the product to the store's computer; the code does not contain the price, which may vary. The price is

stored in a file that can be accessed by the computer. (Obviously, it is easier to change the price once in the computer than to have to repeatedly restamp the price on each can of corn.) The computer automatically tells the point- of-sale terminal what the price is; a printer prints the item description and price on a paper tape for the customer. Some supermarkets are moving to self-scanning, putting the bar code reader-as well as the bagging-in the customer's hands.

Although bar codes were once found primarily in supermarkets, there are a variety of other interesting applications. Bar coding has been described as an inexpensive and remarkably reliable way to get data into a computer. It is no wonder that virtually every industry has found a niche for bar codes. In Brisbane, Australia, bar codes help the Red Cross manage their blood bank inventory. Also consider the case of Federal Express. The management attributes a large part of the corporation's success to the bar-coding system it uses to track packages. Each package is uniquely identified by a ten-digit bar code, which is input to the computer at each point as the package travels through the system. An employee can use a computer terminal to query the location of a given shipment at any time; the sender can request a status report on a package and receive a response within 30 minutes. The figures are impressive: In regard to controlling packages, the company has an accuracy rate of better than 99 percent.

Handwritten Characters

Machines that can read handwritten characters are yet another means of reducing the number of intermediate steps between capturing data and processing it. In many instances it is preferable to write the data and immediately have it usable for processing rather than having data entry operators key it in later. However, not just any kind of handwritten scrawl will do; the rules as to the size, completeness, and legibility of the handwriting are fairly rigid.

Imaging

In a process called imaging, a scanner converts a drawing, a picture, or any document into computer-recognizable form by shining a light on the image and sensing the intensity of the reflection at each point of the image. Scanners come in both handheld and desktop models. The electronic version of the image can then be stored, probably on disk, and reproduced on screen when needed. Businesses find imaging particularly useful for documents, since they can view an exact replica of the original document at any time. If a text image is run through an optical character recognition (OCR) program, then all words and numbers can be manipulated by word processing and other software. The Internal Revenue Service, using imaging and also OCR software that can recognize characters from the image, is now scanning 17,000 tax returns per hour, a significant improvement over hand processing.

Another way to keep photos computer accessible is to have film that was shot with a conventional camera processed onto optical disk instead of prints or slides. Professional photo agencies keep thousands of images on file, ready to be leased for a fee. Typically, a couple of dozen thumbnail-size images can be displayed on the screen at one time; a particular image can be enlarged to full-screen size with a click of a mouse button.

Data Collection Devices
Another source of direct data entry is a data collection device, which may be located in a warehouse or factory or wherever the activity that is generating the data is located. As we noted earlier in the chapter, for example, factory employees can use a plastic card to punch job data directly into a computerized time clock. This process eliminates intermediate steps and ensures that the data will be more accurate.

Data collection devices must be sturdy, trouble-free, and easy to use because they are often located in dusty, humid, or hot or cold locations. They are used by people such as warehouse workers, packers, forklift operators, and others whose primary work is not clerical. Examples of remote data collection devices are machines for taking inventory, reading shipping labels, and recording job costs.

Voice Input
Does your computer have ears? Speaking to a computer, known as voice input or speech recognition, is another form of source input. Speech recognition devices accept the spoken word through a microphone and convert it into binary code (0s and 1s) that can be understood by the computer. Originally, typical users were those with "busy hands," or hands too dirty for the keyboard, or with no access to a keyboard. Such uses are changing radio frequencies in airplane

cockpits, controlling inventory in an auto junkyard, reporting analysis of pathology slides viewed under a microscope, asking for stock-market quotations over the phone, inspecting items moving along an assembly line, and allowing physically disabled users to issue commands.

Most speech recognition systems are speaker-dependent; that is, they must be separately trained for each individual user. The speech recognition system "learns" the voice of the user, who speaks isolated words repeatedly. The voiced words the system "knows" are then recognizable in the future.

Speech recognition systems that are limited to isolated words are called discrete word systems, and users must pause between words. Experts have tagged speech recognition as one of the most difficult things for a computer to do. Eventually, continuous word systems will be able to interpret sustained speech, so users can speak normally; so far, such systems are limited by vocabulary to a single subject, such as insurance or the weather. A key advantage of delivering input to a computer in a normal speaking pattern is ease of use. Such systems may also be propelled by the explosion of hand and wrist ailments associated with extensive computer keying. Today, software is available to let computers take dictation from people who are willing to pause . . . briefly . . . between . . . words; the best systems are quite accurate and equivalent to typing 70 words per minute.

Touch Screens
One way of getting input directly from the source is to have a human simply point to a selection. The edges of the monitor of a touch screen emit horizontal and vertical beams of light that criss-cross the screen. When a finger touches the screen, the interrupted light beams can pinpoint the location selected on the screen. Kiosks in public places such as malls offer a variety of services via touch screens. An insurance company kiosk will let you select a policy or a government kiosk will let you order a copy of your birth certificate. Kiosks are also found in private stores. Wal-Mart, for example, uses a kiosk to let customers find needed auto parts. Many delicatessens let you point to salami on rye, among the other selections.

Delivering input to a computer by simply looking at the computer would seem to be the ultimate in capturing data at the source. The principles are reminiscent of making a screen selection by touching the screen with the finger. Electrodes attached to the skin around the eyes respond to movement of the eye muscles, which produce tiny electric signals when they contract. The signals are read by the computer system, which determines the location on the screen where the user is looking.

Such a system is not yet the mainstream. The first people to benefit would likely be those who, due to disabilities or busyness, cannot use their hands or voices for input.

1.4 Output: Information for the User

As we have seen, computer output takes the form of screen or printer output. Other forms of output include voice, microfilm, and various forms of graphics output.

A computer system often is designed to produce several kinds of output. An example is a travel agency that uses a computer system. If a customer asks about airline connections to Toronto, Calgary, and Vancouver, say, the travel agent will probably make a few queries to the system to receive on-screen output indicating availability on the various flights. After the reservations have been confirmed, the agent can ask for printed output that includes the tickets, the traveler's itinerary, and the invoice. The agency may also keep the customer records on microfilm. In addition, agency management may periodically receive printed reports and charts, such as monthly summaries of sales figures or pie charts of regional costs. We begin with the most common form of output, computer screens.

Computer Screen Technology

A user's first interaction with a computer screen may be the screen response to the user's input. When data is entered, it appears on the screen. Furthermore, the computer response to that data-the output-also appears on the screen. Computer screens come in many varieties, but the most common kind is the cathode ray tube (CRT). Most CRT screens use a technology called raster-scan technology. The backing of the screen display has a phosphorous coating, which will glow whenever it is hit by a beam of electrons. But the light does not stay lit very long, so the image must be refreshed often. If the screen is not refreshed often enough, the fading screen image appears to flicker. A scan rate-the number of times the screen is refreshed-of 60 times per second is usually adequate to retain a clear screen image. As the user, you tell the computer what image you want on the screen, by typing, say, the letter M, and the computer sends the appropriate image to be beamed on the screen. This is essentially the same process used to produce television images.

A computer display screen that can be used for graphics is divided into dots that are called addressable, because they can be addressed individually by the graphics software. Each dot can be illuminated individually on the screen. Each dot is potentially a picture element, or pixel. The resolution of the screen, its clarity, is directly related to the number of pixels on the screen: The more pixels, the higher the resolution. Some computers come with built-in graphics capability. Others need a device, called a graphics card or graphics adapter board, that has to be added.

There have been several color screen standards, relating particularly to resolution. The first color display was CGA (color graphics adapter), which had low resolution by today's standards (320x200 pixels). This was followed by the sharper EGA (enhanced graphics adapter), featuring 640x350 pixels. Today, VGA and SVGA are common standards. VGA (video graphics array) has 640x480 pixels. SVGA (super VGA) offers 800x600 pixels or 1024x768 pixels, by far the superior clarity.

Is bigger really better? Screen sizes are measured diagonally. Many personal computers come with a 15 inch screen. A 15 inch screen is fine for most single applications, but for applications with large graphics, or for having multiple windows open, it is sometimes inadequate. For a few hundred dollars more, 17 inch can be better. There are even bigger screens that cost substantially more. Bigger is usually better, but more expensive.

Types of Screens

Cathode ray tube monitors that display text and graphics are in common use today. Although most CRTs are color, some screens are monochrome, meaning only one color, usually green, appears on a dark background. Another type of screen technology is the liquid crystal display (LCD), a flat display often seen on watches and calculators. LCD screens are used on laptop computers. Some LCDs are monochrome, but color screens are popular. Some laptop screens are nearing CRTs in resolution quality.

Terminals

A screen may be the monitor of a self-contained personal computer, or it may be part of a terminal that is one of many terminals attached to a large computer. A terminal consists of an input device, an output device, and a communications link to the main computer. Most commonly, a terminal has a keyboard for an input device and a screen for an output device, although there are many variations on this theme.

Printers

A printer is a device that produces printed paper output, known in the computer industry as hard copy because it is tangible and permanent (unlike soft copy, which is displayed on a screen). Some printers produce only letters and numbers, whereas others can also produce graphics.

Letters and numbers are formed by a printer either as solid characters or as dot-matrix characters. Dot-matrix printers create characters in the same way that individual lights in a pattern spell out words on a basketball scoreboard. Dot-matrix printers construct a character by activating a matrix of pins that produce the shape of the character. A traditional matrix is 5x7-that is, five dots wide and seven dots high. These printers are sometimes called 9-pin printers, because they have two extra vertical dots for descenders on the lowercase letters g, j, p, and y. The 24-pin dot-matrix printer, which uses a series of overlapping dots, dominates the dot-matrix market. The more dots, the better the quality of the character produced. Some dot-matrix printers can produce color images.

There are two ways of printing an image on paper: the impact method and the non-impact method. Let us take a closer look at the difference.

Impact Printers

The term impact refers to the fact that impact printers use some sort of physical contact with the paper to produce an image, physically striking paper, ribbon, and print hammer together. The impact may be produced by a print hammer character, like that of a typewriter key striking a ribbon against the paper, or by a print hammer hitting paper and ribbon against a character. A dot-matrix printer is one example of an impact printer. High- quality impact printers print only one character at a time.

However, users who are more concerned about high volume than high quality usually use line printers - impact printers that print an entire line at a time. Organizations that use mainframe and minicomputers usually have several line printers. Such organizations are likely to print hearty reports, perhaps relating to payroll or costs, for internal use. The volume of the report and the fact that it will not be seen by customers makes the speedy-and less expensive line printer appropriate. One final note about impact printers: An impact printer must be used if printing a multiple-copy report so that the duplicate copies will receive the imprint.

Non-impact Printers
A non-impact printer places an image on a page without physically touching the page. The major technologies competing in the non-impact market are laser and ink-jet. Laser printers use a light beam to help transfer images to paper, producing extremely high-quality results. Laser printers print a page at a time at impressive speeds. Large organizations use laser printers to produce high-volume customer-oriented reports. At the personal computer end, low-end black and white laser printers can now be purchased for a few hundred dollars. However, color laser jet printers are more expensive.

The rush to laser printers has been influenced by the trend toward desktop publishing-using a personal computer, a laser printer, and special software to make professional-looking publications, such as newsletters.

Ink-jet printers, by spraying ink from multiple jet nozzles, can print both black and white and in several different colors of ink to produce excellent graphics. As good as they are, color printers are not perfect. The color you see on your computer screen is not necessarily the color you will see on the printed output. Nor is it likely to be the color you would see on a four-color offset printing press. Nevertheless, with low-end printers now under $250, they may be a bargain for users who want their own color output capability.

There are many advantages to non-impact printers over impact ones, but there are two major reasons for their growing popularity: They are faster and quieter. Other advantages of non-impact printers over conventional mechanical printers are their ability to change typefaces automatically and their ability to produce high-quality graphics.

Voice Output

We have already examined voice input in some detail. As you will see in this section, however, computers are frequently like people in the sense that they find it easier to talk than to listen. Speech synthesis is the process of enabling machines to talk to people is much easier than speech recognition. "The key is in the ignition," your car says to you as you open the car door to get out. Machine voices are not real human voices. They are the product of voice synthesizers (also called voice-output devices or audio-response units), which convert data in main storage to vocalized sounds understandable to humans.

There are two basic approaches to getting a computer to talk. The first is synthesis by analysis, in which the device analyzes the input of an actual human voice speaking words, stores and processes the spoken sounds, and reproduces them as needed. The process of storing words is similar to the digitizing process we discussed earlier when considering voice input. In essence, synthesis by analysis uses the computer as a digital tape recorder.

The second approach to synthesizing speech is synthesis by rule, in which the device applies a complex set of linguistic rules to create artificial speech. Synthesis based on the human voice has the advantage of sounding more natural, but it is limited to the number of words stored in the computer.

Voice output has become common in such places as airline and bus terminals, banks, and brokerage houses. It is typically used when an inquiry is followed by a short reply (such as a bank balance or flight time). Many businesses have found other creative uses for voice output as it applies to the telephone. Automatic telephone voices ("Hello, this is a computer speaking. . . ") take surveys, inform customers that catalog orders are ready to be picked up, and, perhaps, remind consumers that they have not paid their bills.

Music Output

Personal computer users have occasionally sent primitive musical messages, feeble tones that wheezed from the tiny internal speaker. Many users remain at this level, but a significant change is in progress.

Professional musicians lead the way, using special sound chips that simulate different instruments. A sound card, installed internally in the computer, and attached speakers complete the output environment. Now, using appropriate software, the computer can produce the sound of an orchestra or a rock band. Those of us who simply enjoy music can have a full sight/sound experience using multimedia, which we will explore in detail in the next chapter.

1.5 Computer Graphics

Let us take a moment to glimpse everyone's favorite, computer graphics. Just about everyone has seen TV commercials or movies that use computer-produced animated graphics. Computer graphics can also be found in education, computer art, science, sports, and more. But perhaps their most prevalent use today is in business.

Business Graphics

It might seem wasteful to use color graphics to display what could more inexpensively be shown to managers as numbers in standard computer printouts. However, colorful graphics, maps, and charts can help managers compare data more easily, spot trends, and make decisions more quickly. Also, the use of color helps people get the picture-literally. Finally, although color graphs and charts have been used in business for years-usually to make presentations to higher management or outside clients-the computer allows them to be rendered quickly, before information becomes outdated. One user refers to business graphics as "computer- assisted insight."

Video Graphics

Video graphics can be as creative as an animated cartoon. Although they operate on the same principle as a moving picture or cartoon-one frame at a time in quick succession video graphics are produced by computers. Video graphics have made their biggest splash on television, but many people do not realize they are watching a computer at work. The next time you watch television, skip the trip to the kitchen and pay special attention to the commercials. Unless there is a live human in the advertisement, there is a good chance that the moving objects you see, such as floating cars and bobbing electric razors, are computer output. Another fertile ground for video graphics is a television network's logo and theme. Accompanied by music and swooshing sounds, the network symbol spins and cavorts and turns itself inside out, all with the finesse that only a computer could supply.

Computer-Aided Design/Computer-Aided Manufacturing

For more than a decade, computer graphics have also been part and parcel of a field known by the abbreviation CAD/CAM-short for computer- aided design/computer-aided manufacturing. In this area computers are used to create two- and three-dimensional pictures of everything from hand tools to tractors. CAD/CAM provides a bridge between design (planning what a product will be) and manufacturing (actually making the planned product). As a manager at Chrysler said, "Many companies have design data and manufacturing data, and the two are never the same. At Chrysler, we have only one set of data that everyone dips into." Keeping data in one place, of course, makes changes easier and encourages consistency.

Graphics Input Devices

There are many ways to produce and interact with screen graphics. We have already described the mouse; the following are some other common devices that allow the user to interact with screen graphics. A digitizing tablet lets you create your own images. This device has a special stylus that you can use to draw or trace images, which are then converted to digital data that can be processed by the computer.

For direct interaction with your computer screen, the light pen is ideal. It is versatile enough to modify screen graphics or make a menu selection-that is, to choose from a list of activity choices on the screen. A light pen has a light-sensitive cell at one end. When you place the light pen against the screen, it closes a photoelectric circuit that pinpoints the spot the pen is touching. This tells the computer where to enter or modify pictures or data on the screen.

Finally, a well-known graphics input device is the joystick, dear to the hearts of video game fans. This device allows fingertip control of figures on a CRT screen.

Graphics Output Devices

Just as there are many different ways to input graphics to the computer, there are many different ways to output graphics. Graphics are most commonly output on a screen or printed paper, as previously discussed. Another popular graphics output device is the plotter, which can draw hard-copy graphics output in the form of maps, bar charts, engineering drawings, and even two- or three-dimensional illustrations. Plotters often come with a set of four pens in four different colors. Most plotters also offer shading features.

New forms of computer input and output are announced regularly, often with promises of multiple benefits and new ease of use. Part of the excitement of the computer world is that these promises are usually kept, and users reap the benefits directly. Input and output just keep getting better.

In the subsequent chapters, we will review some current research trends related to computer systems.

2. MASSIVE MULTIPLAYER ONLINE GAMES

Online games give the player the ability to compete against other players over a network. The massively multiplayer online game is a type of online computer game that enables hundreds or thousands of players from various parts of the world to simultaneously interact in a gaming environment they are connected to via the network. Game designers have successfully built multiplayer (MP) and massively multiplayer online games (MMOG) using different approaches. MMOGs were first introduced by various companies as Massive Multiplayer Online Role Playing Game (MMORPG).

A key difference between the multi-player (MP) online game and MMOG suggested in is scale and the associated infrastructure to support it. In MP games, the numbers of concurrent players are between 16 and 32. The game can be played either stand-alone or in multiplayer-network mode, and one of the players machines acts as the server. The game duration is short-lived and if the server crashes, the game is severely disrupted. Today MMOG's, with hundreds of thousands of players online at the same time; also span hundreds of servers. Game session must last for a long time requiring it to be run on dedicated servers equipped with a persistent database. Network bandwidth to support the game-related traffic also comes with a cost. High bandwidth also a means to have better and high quality graphics support. High quality graphics can result in attracting more and more users, thus creating massive user environment. MMOGs have in the past years grown into a million player industry worldwide, especially in Asia, Europe and North America earning massive profit. If more visualization effects and graphics can be added in MMOG, not only more users can be attracted from all over the World but also can lift the profit to another level.

MMOG's are played on network (internet, for example) and computers use protocols to communicate with each other on internet. So choice of protocol is subtle for efficient use of bandwidth. Well known family of protocols belong to TCP/IP family and each protocol solves problems related to its on layer. For the specific requirements of MMOG, it is needed to select a suitable transport layer protocol to provide the exact functionalities required, thus eliminating any overhead that may affect the performance. An example scenario would be like; TCP provide reliable data transfer but can affect the performance due to unnecessary retransmissions in some cases. Choice of protocol for the presented architecture would be described in more detail in one of the upcoming section. Strict timing constraint for state handling is critical issue too. This is essentially a QoS concern. Very important to a multiplayer game, is the problem of maintaining the same game state information on each of the player's instance of the game and generating the effect of each player belonging to the same game instance. This concern affects the choice of middleware for the architecture. We proposed data distribution standard as middleware having native support to meet this constraint.

In this chapter we discuss a loosely coupled, service oriented architecture mainly to overcome the above mentioned challenges. We have proposed a specific middleware (based on open source DDS) to add all the above said functionalities in MMOG's at real time and modelled simulation flow in business process executed language (BPEL). Most important technical contribution towards design are the service oriented architectural concepts and data centric publish subscribe middleware. The need for presenting this study arises because current architectures for online gaming applications do not meet scalability requirements and do not provide QoS guarantees. Client-server architecture cannot be assumed to bear load of such a large number of users of MMOG's. Mirrored client-server architecture uses a synchronization technique which is difficult to maintain when large numbers of players are online in MMOG and the environment has become highly dynamic. In addition since each server has a local copy of whole game state, when network becomes highly scalable, additional resources may be needed on the server for brisk processing capabilities. Peer to peer gaming is also less reliable in terms of security as global game state is stored in local peer, hence malicious peers can modify the game state and propagate to other peers.

2.1 Service oriented architecture

Service-oriented architecture (SOA) provides methods for independent and incremental development and integration of systems. Systems typically assume functionality around business processes and package them as interoperable "services". SOA also describes an information infrastructure which allows different applications to exchange data with one another as they participate in the related process. Service Oriented Architecture ensures functionalities like:

• Interoperability among the systems having different software

• Reusability of network resources

• Seamless flow of data from one side to other

• Monitoring and tracking of the information

• Scalability of the already deployed network

This standardized architecture is designed to better support the connection of various systems of systems and the sharing of data. It breaks down large applications into smaller modules as services and unifies different processes. Different groups of people both inside and outside of system can use these applications. Data flow architecture, Event driven architecture and client server architecture are basic date orchestration approaches used by any service oriented architecture. The basic requirement of any real time service oriented architecture is to ensure the quality of service. Real time service oriented architecture provides real time system operations and interaction between services and provides support to meet with strict timing constraints.

2.2 SOA for MMOG

An SQL based database holds the user attributes such as user login, password, account information and user privilege as shown in table 1.

2.2.1 SQL queries

SQL queries to create tables, populate the database and retrieve records are as follows.

2.2.2. Creating database

```
CREATE DATABASE game_data;
```

2.2.3. Creating tables

```
CREATE TABLE user_accounts
(user_login VARCHAR(25) NOT NULL,
```

password VARCHAR(25) NOT NULL,

user_privillage VARCHAR(25) NOT NULL,

account_creation_date DATE,

account_expiration_date DATE);

Table 1: An SQL based database holds the user attributes

user_login	password	user_privilege	account_creation_date	account_expiration_date
Max	*******	FULL	09/10/2008	09/10/2014
John123	******	BASIC	05/11/2008	05/11/2013
.				
.				
.				

2.2.4. Populating tables

INSERT INTO user_accounts ('Max', 'game123', 'Full', '09/10/2008', '09/10/2014');

INSERT INTO user_accounts ('John123', 'helloworld', 'basic', '05/11/2008', '05/11/2013');

2.2.5. Retrieving records

SELECT user_privilege, account_expiration_date

FROM user_accounts

WHERE user_login == 'Max'

2.2.6 Account login server

This server deals with the information related to the user account. Main purpose of this server is to take login data input from the user side, authenticate user using account database, communicate with the billing and Game servers.

2.2.7. Account billing server

BPEL/XML based server that keep track of user billing information.

2.2.8. Game server

It is a simple online game server that allows user to play single player or multiplayer games.

2.2.9. Auxiliary services server

It can be used to keep track of user's auxiliary actions like chatting. It can also be a part of Game Server.

2.3. Simulation of SOA concept for servers

Traditional implementation of these standalone servers is done by simple HTML and PHP scripting with a centralized database. We propose to use a loosely coupled, service oriented implementation for these services as part of MMOG. Advantages achieved through such design components validate the usefulness of our proposed architecture for MMOG [24]. In our presented scenario we have three independent processes that are logically distributed over the network.

i. User Authentication Process
ii. User Check Process
iii. Credit Card Check Process

All the three process have different input output requirements. Processes are implemented using Business Process Execution Language (BPEL). Connection between two different processes is done through logical ports, implemented in Web Service Description Language (WSDL). Such an implementation provides loosely coupled, service oriented scenario.

2.4. Simulation flow in BPEL

Business Process Execution Language (BPEL), short for Web Services Business Process Execution Language (WS-BPEL) is an executable language for specifying interactions with Web Services. It has widely become an XML based standard for defining business processes. Business Process Execution Language supports processes which exchange (export and import) information by using Web Service interfaces exclusively. BPEL essentially has a very rich expressive power for describing the behavior of business processes and support service oriented paradigm. Use of BPEL for the composition and implementation of above mentioned process, ensures many functionalities. This provides loose coupling through operations that exchange data only. This differs from component and distributed object models, where behavior can also be exchanged. Operations in these web services based on the exchange of XML data. They are a collection of input, output, and fault messages. The combination of messages defines the type of operation. This differs from previous distributed technologies. It has also support for asynchronous as well as synchronous interactions. It allows information exchange in a stateless manner.

BPEL can be used for real time service oriented architecture (RTSOA) for some business processes where real time requirement is not very tight. The processes which have hard real time requirements cannot be handle by BPEL as it does not have the required capabilities. In our MMOG problem we require more than soft real time which cannot be provided by BPEL. Therefore we have presented a specific middleware to fulfil these requirements.

'UserApproveService' process invokes two other processes, which performs username authentication and credit card authentication without having dependency upon each other. 'UserCheckService' process is invoked by the main process 'UserApproveService' for authentication. Similarly 'CardCheckProcess' is also invoked by 'UserApproveService' and returns a positive message if approved and negative response if denied. Then 'userApproveService' makes decisions based on messages provided by other two services. All the processes are deployed over a local GlassFishV2 server. User Approve Service process invokes two other processes, which performs username authentication and credit card authentication without having dependency upon each other. Also there is no centralized database as was the case with previous implementation with PHP and SQL. UserCheckService process is invoked by the main process 'UserApproveService' for authentication and returns the positive reply if information matches and negative reply if credentials don't match.

2.5. Middle-ware for MMOG

For the architecture proposed, middleware is the backbone and choice for this determines the overall reach of the complete architecture. BPEL can prove to be a good choice, as we described in user authentication services. Advantage of using BPEL is a very low deployment cost of the system. Problem with such implementation is the ability of BPEL to support only soft real time processes. As mentioned in previous section, MMOGs may require more than soft real time capability. For a robust solution to this problem we propose to use an open source 'Data Distribution Service (DDS) Standard' from the Object Management Group (OMG), as a middleware. This standard defines an efficient, high performance publish-subscribe system that offers a predictable way of meeting the data-distribution requirements of data-critical systems with minimal overhead.

In networked massive multiplayer gaming scenario, due to the scalability limits and single point-of failure topologies of traditional client/server architectures, DDS specifies an information hub to which game applications at end users can dynamically connect in order to publish and subscribe to information. In contrast to most network games present today, which follows predefined, well implemented protocols like TCP, our gaming architecture must be following the same promises as delivered by DDS middleware as part of real time service oriented architecture. The promises to be delivered are:

1) Data Centric Communication Exchange: Communication network model of game is pure data-centric exchange as required by RTSOA data oriented paradigm. Gaming application, at top layer publishes data, which is then made available to other remote users that are interested in it. In case of at most two players, publisher on one side publishes data and subscriber on other side use it for its application layer and vice versa. This allows communication exchange as pure data centric.

2) QoS Policies: We achieve the required flexibility by this communication exchange. Middleware specifies the available resources and provides policies to ensure the availability of resources to meet the most critical requirements. In this way Quality of Service (QoS) property that affect predictability, overhead, and resource utilization can be controlled. That allows game users to exchange data with good QoS achievable.

3) Scalability: Since scalability as another important issue in multiplayer online games, by building DDS as a middleware in gaming communication network, we promise the system to scale to multiple users having their own publishers and subscribers in a robust manner. A comparison between existing middleware technologies is given in table 2.

Table 2. Comparing DDS with other Technologies

Technology	Requirement			
	Non Real Time	**Soft Real Time**	**Hard Real Time**	**Extreme Real Time**
DCOM	Yes	No	No	No
JAVA/RMI	Yes	Yes	No	No
CORBA	Yes	Yes	Yes	No
DDS	Yes	Yes	Yes	Yes
MPI	No	No	No	Yes

2.6. MMOG requirements and solutions

As mentioned in section 2.4, different standards claim for the provision of RTSOA. Choice of data distribution standard is justified since not only it can handle RTSOA but can also be used to address many issues specific to MMOGs. In the following we discuss the additional support provided by the middleware system to address common issues that must be resolved in order to achieve a realistic MMOG behaviour. One of the major issues associated with MMOG is its scalability and communication performance that enables the interactive system to maintain the quality and coordination of the game experience. Scalability means, the ability of a system to respond to an increasing demand from its users, without significantly degrading the quality of the interactive experience. This is overall an architecture that enables the integration of new components, resources and technologies for system expandability. This architecture is service oriented in nature and it maintains loosely coupled entities. In loosely coupled paradigm all entities are independent and support scalability. The quality and coordination of communication performance is achieved by QOS block of Data Distribution Service. MMOGs are typically migrating towards 3D environment for player's interaction. These environments can become quiet dynamic, making it impossible for the clients to save the virtual world state hoping that when the player returns the game state remains the same. Presence of history policy as a part of QOS Block in this architecture can address issues related to state handling of the game.

MMOG requires different multimedia (Audio, video, text) objects; efficient temporal presentation of these is an important question. Proposed middleware can handle issues related to presentation of multimedia objects by using presentation policy in the QOS Block. For a single instant of game when having multiple users (a group of users), there arises a need for a policy to handle group based data. To handle group based data the middleware has in built Group Data policy in QOS block. Group data policy along with Data Reader Listener and Data Writer Listener provide policies to manage group data. If we have multiple changes in some object by different users than we need to send the coherent changes to appropriate users; this can be managed in presentation policy provided by DDS. To meet the requirement of reliable data service in MMOG, reliability policy present in QOS block of the middleware can be implemented. MMOG requires smooth playback even in the presence of network latency or delay. Network Latency should not block the game from updating for an unnecessary long time. It is highly undesirable to continue the game after a reply message arrives. Suspend and Resume publication policies in a publisher block used by DDS, can handle this situation.

In MMOG different users can join or leave the game. A good middleware should detect the arrival or departure of clients. In DDS we have Delete publisher, Create Publisher, Delete Subscriber and Create Subscriber policies to handle the issue of arrival and departure of users. In MMOG virtual environment can become quite big, and a significant part of it is not relevant to the action context of a player at a certain time. Therefore each player does not need to receive notice of all the changes that are happening everywhere else in the virtual environment. Support for such kind of scenario can be provided by event filtering policy to subscribe only to the data which is relevant to a particular user. The problem of maintaining the same game state information on each of the player's instance of the game and generating the effect to other players is quite subtle. For example in a shooting game (likewise in racing game) the exact positions of all the player's characters must be represented on the player's screens at the same time. If there was a delay in the updating of the position of the characters then two players may have wrong game state displayed on their screens which in turn may end with wrong results not in accordance with player's actions. Similarly in racing game this may result in a scenario that both player's car are at first position as perceived by players. In the middleware QoS Policy block have 'Listener' and 'Status' interfaces. 'Listener' provide a mechanism for the service to asynchronously inform the application of relevant changes in the communication status and 'Status' represents the communication status of the players. Change in status values asynchronously informs the application through these interfaces.

Because of the growing broadband network, multi-player online games can be played while interacting with the other players and without meeting them. Here are some pros and cons of multiplayer online games. Online games provide privacy. We need not to reveal the true identity to other users while maintaining interaction with them. Online games are cheaper because it can be played from the comfort of our time playing for as long as we want.

Massive multi-player online games are not early to be finished and these are time consuming. These games are quite competitive and the players need time to think of strategies to accomplish their goals. In general these role playing games lessen social interaction. Because of the large amount of time players spend, interacting with other players mostly through chat, they become impersonal in dealing with people in real life. SOA for MMOG will require a large investment by way of technology, development and trained staff. We discuss the limitations of SOA deployment below.

1) Since services described in section 2.4, invoke other services, each service needs to validate completely every input parameter. This may have negative impact on response time.

2) Any malicious activity introduced in a well-used service may take out the entire application, at some times.

3) When using data distribution service (DDS), an open standard middleware, a service is much more open to other services and applications and thus security becomes an issue.

4) Service management becomes an issue since SOA blurs the boundaries of application ownership. It has been recommended in that a multi-gaming-vendor solution can fully benefit from the flexible nature of SOA.

Open source implementation of the Data Distribution Standard as middleware is still a technical challenge. Hierarchical design of the standard will require proper integration with the application and specific algorithms for various functionalities which needs to be explored as an open research issue. Current work also needs to be extended to increase the flexibility of resource allocation. In an MMOG cloud environment, virtual machines (VMs) in game servers are allocated to serve players. SOA based MMOGs can also be integrated with cloud computing architectures for efficient resource allocation and a cost effective solution.

MMOG architecture require much more than classic tightly coupled distributed services. In this paper we have proposed a service oriented architecture for the deployment of MMOGs. Such architecture provides loosely coupled distributed services. Taking it a step further, we also considered real time requirements for such applications. Our proposed architecture achieves much of its capabilities from an underline middleware and ensures both service oriented and real time requirements. For the scheme presented in this paper we considered DDS standard as middleware. DDS standard has shown success in various proprietary applications having critical RTSO requirements. To demonstrate the capabilities of our proposed loosely coupled service oriented architecture, we implemented a prototype using business process execution language. The ease with which a new process can integrate in the implemented prototype and level of independence available to the processes, show the usefulness of such architecture.

Effectiveness of the proposed architecture highly depends on the choice of middleware. Open source implementation of the Data Distribution Standard as middleware is not yet available. Hierarchical design of the standard will require proper integration with the application and specific algorithms for various functionalities. Further, software models using service oriented concepts for MMOG can be developed and implemented as a software package. Effective resource allocation and cost effective solutions as well as scheduling algorithms for anycast and multicast routing on underlying network layer protocols need to be investigated.

3. SOFTWARE SYSTEMS AND COST ESTIMATION

Software cost estimation is a critical stage that is being done in the initial phases of software development process. The aim of such a process is to have a better future sight of the project progress and its phases. Another main objective is to have clear project details and specifications to assist stakeholders in managing the project in terms of human resources, assets, software, data and even in the feasibility study. Accurate estimation results with definitely helps the project manager to do better estimation for the project cost, the time required for various project phases and resources or assets. However, the inaccuracy may result from the project cost estimation process that will certainly affect the project delivery. A project with wrong or imprecision evaluation will face issues with delivery timing, resources required, budget or even in quality or operational side and sometimes the project may fail or aborted. Hence, the cost estimation is a significant part of the software projects and so it continues to be a complex issue in the software engineering field. Therefore, many studies and researches have been conducted for the purpose of enhancing and improving the estimation process and get more accurate and dependable results.

On the other hand, recently machine learning (ML) techniques become very essential in software studies. In many scientific researches, ML methods are being used and executed most likely in the various fields, however, depending on the research nature and objectives one or more of the methods will be selected. As the process of software cost estimation is rapidly evolving which may include technology advances, team skills and experience, and tools and programming languages available, it gives superiority to ML techniques than some other methods that may stick to statistical and mathematical work. Hence, ML can be a suitable technique to build the proposed model due to the ability to learn from historical data and adapt the wide variations that join software project development. In this work, ML techniques will be used to evaluate and compare the results of implementing such techniques on datasets. Dataset will be collected from the public that available on internet called Upsp05 and Upsp05-tf that contains practical software engineering data. Datasets can be downloaded from (http://tunedit.org/repo/promise/effortprediction) which is made publicly available to encourage and improve the cost estimation work in software engineering.

By applying ML methods on the dataset, it can be concluded if the ML techniques could be applied successfully on software cost estimation data or not. If yes, it would be possible to know which method scored the best results and also it is likely to decide if an ML model can be developed to evaluate and estimate the software cost.

Many studies proposed different models for estimating software cost. Several models have proposed and built to find alternatives, enhance or support existing models. Constructive cost model (COCOMO) is considered as one of the most known models in the field of software cost estimation. For the purpose of improving COCOMO II accuracy model proposed a method to optimize the parameters used in COCOMO II model. The proposed model is capable of candling improper and unclear inputs in an efficient way and so improves software reliability. In 2011, a study aimed to examine the results of applying fuzzy logic on COCOMO II and FL-COCOMO II and its effect on cost estimation. The research focused on SCE model and incorporating fuzzy logic to assess the inaccuracy of software attributes. The study' outcomes showed from applying various datasets that FL-COCOMO II model scored better estimation outcomes than the COCOMO II based on different assessment criteria.

Litoriya, et al. conducted an analysis of the cost drivers that affect directly the cost estimation model accuracy and a substitution process has done for those drivers with nearest values to show and prove the decrease in the software cost using Agile COCOMO II. In 2017, Saljoughinejad and Khatibi proposed a new study based on COCOMO model to enhance and improve the accuracy of the software cost estimation process. The COCOMO model has been selected due to its flexibility and applicability to various types of projects. During the study, an analysis of cost drivers has been done using different meta-heuristic algorithms. The improvement process was based on the effective selection of the factors and coefficients used in the model. The improvement was on comprises cost drivers and coefficients estimations. Results showed that explicit superiority once a comparison is done between the proposed model and COCOMO or other models. Chen, et al. focused on software cost estimation using different models such as COCOMO and how it can be improved by using the WRAPPER feature in DM. It is basically depending on feature subset selection (FSS), where it concentrates on mainly the most promising fields in the dataset and neglects the other to speed up the processing time. So by using the WRAPPER feature, they concluded that COCOMO model can be improved and its results could be more efficient. Khalifelu and Gharehchopogh presented various software cost estimation models founded on data mining methods for the purpose of choosing appropriate Artificial intelligence (AI) techniques that are needed in new projects. Their main aim of all experiments was to asset and compare different data mining approaches with intermediate COCOMO models with respect to the prediction's accuracy. The achieved results were promised and noticeable.

Beside many researches done on the COCOMO model and how to enhance it, there are other studies conducted trying to propose new models and algorithms that may add value to the field. Whigham, et al. suggested a baseline model that is essential to be used for all projects that are being developed and software effort estimation study is required. It is very important to compare the results with the baseline when a new or existing method is carried out to examine the prediction process. Their proposed model called automatic transformations linear model (ATLM) that could be used as a baseline for the comparison process between the software effort estimation methods.

Sarro, et al. introduced a new effort estimation algorithm that is based on a combination of confidence interval analysis and assessment of the mean absolute error (MAE). The developed algorithm has been tested and evaluated based on three different factors, however, the results were very promised. The experiments were done on the dataset that is collected from more than 700 software projects. Recently, Masoudi-Sobhanzadeh, et al. model can be applied in many fields including designing drug, biology, and image processing. The model starts by selecting a subset of features/factors based on optimizations algorisms to be transmitted later to the classifiers or learners. The learners are SVM, ANN and Decision Tree, which can be applied to regressions and classification datasets. Two types of optimization algorithms and the three classifiers can be applied by researchers to any dataset to use this model which is called *FeatureSelect*. The *FeatureSelect* has been tested on 8 different datasets in size and nature were great results have been observed.

On the other hand, machine learning algorithms considered to be vital in nowadays studies. ML techniques are widely used and their outcome results are dependable and reliable in many researches. In 2018, a deep study did an analysis of 25 releases containing hundreds of classes to test the effort indicators. The study concluded that out of 18 machine learning algorithms used, IBk, KStar, Additive Regression, and Multi-Layer Perceptron were capable to estimate the test effort precisely. Moreover, the work in Khalid, et al. proposed a prediction model to estimate the duration of the software processes using ML algorithms. Two training models which are Levenberg–Marquardt (LM) and Bayesian regularization back propagation (BR) used to test and evaluate FFNN and RBNN algorithms. The comparison between the two models showed that BR outcomes are slightly better. Also, BR is more desirable as its application is cost effective. Yeh and Deng proposed a framework to predict the software product life cycle using two machine learning algorithms. The work presented a more precise and generalizable model for product cost estimation.

In 2019, research has been done on breast cancer trying to build models for visualizing and detecting analytical signs of breast cancer survival rate using ML algorithms. To determine the important aspects of breast cancer survival rate, prediction algorithms were developed using the extreme boost, decision tree, neural networks, random forest support vector machine, and logistic regression. All the algorithms scored very high and close outcomes and the highest one was random forest which can be concluded that those methods could be used as predictive models in breast cancer studies. Some major challenges usually evolve software cost estimation process such as factors related to technology and creativity. In addition, some uncertain problems can happen during the implementation like lack of resources or increasing the cost of OS. Due to that, Kumari and Pushkar introduced a hybrid algorithm to better estimate the SCE based on a combination of COA-Cuckoo and KNN. The hybrid algorithm runs on 6 different datasets and evaluated using 8 examined criteria. The overall results show improved accuracy on cost estimation.

Pospieszny, et al. developed an approach based on machine learning algorithms to limit the gap between recent researches and real implementations. The achieved results for the proposed model were very accurate and authors believe that it gives more realistic results in terms of software effort and duration estimation for practical projects. Furthermore, Pandey [16] did an analysis study on most of the techniques and methods used in software cost estimation. He tried to mention some of the main advantages and drawbacks of each one. He concluded that all project factors are important and critical to evaluate and estimate the cost of a project and they can differ in their important and influence from one project to another. The main factors that should be included in estimation metrics are qualitative: team experience, development environment, and culture; quantitative factors are project size and the available resources. Başkeleş, et al. carried out many experiments on software effort estimation using different machine learning methods based on three main dissimilar datasets. As a conclusion, they have noticed that parametric models are inadequate for software effort estimation process.

Some other studies focused more on the cost estimation environment and other related factors like software development cycle associated with each project. For example, in 2018, Rahikkala, et al. introduced a study on the role of the organizational phenomena and how its various factors can improve and influence the process of software cost estimation. Most of the researches focus on the development and improvement of the SCE including technical factors and methodologies without mentioning or analyzing the impact of the environment or organizational factors. By conducting a case study and quantitative research, the authors concluded that senior management responsibility is essential in making a significant estimation, whereas the daily follow up is not required. They also found that no significant individual factors that may affect directly the estimation process. Another work conducted on Agile Development Life Cycle. Due to its high success rates and because of its rapid nature capability to adopt changes, Agile Development Cycle became very popular and widely used since the late 90s. Vyas, et al. did a great job in 2017 by doing a survey to highlight the most trends related to the Agile Software Development (ASD) process and how it relates to the cost estimation. The authors were able to identify the factors to be included or not in the estimation process in order to get a more accurate and true cost for projects.

3.1. Machine Learning Algorithms

In this section, a quick and brief overview is done on the ML methods that have been used in building prediction models.

Random forest is a machine learning algorithm constructed on decision tree algorithms. It operates like a group of constructed decision trees that works independently where each tree is using a distinctive part of the dataset. In each tree, it consists of two randomization levels. The first one is called "bagging" or bootstrap of aggregation and the other level is at each node of the decision tree. REPTree is an abbreviation of Reduced Error Pruning Tree. The tree is being built in a fast and learnable way depending on the gained information. REPTree is another kind of decision trees that uses regression tree, which can create many trees in various rounds or iterations. Then, out of all the generated trees, the best one is being selected. To do the pruning process for the tree, the mean square error is measured based on the tree predictions. M5P method is another tree model that is being constructed based on Quinlan's M5 algorithm. Originally, in addition to adding the linear regression method to the tree leave nodes, M5 model is also based on the conventional decision tree. The trained data is used by the algorithm to form the nodes and represent the decision tree model. The ZeroR algorithm is one of the simplest classifiers. It considers all required potential values and the attributes being targeted. Based on the provided data and using the target attribute, the required output will always be found. This classifier does not have a rule that depends on the untargeted attribute.

The Decision table classifier is a classification model used in prediction studies. Its idea is similar to decision trees or neural networks, where it involves a hierarchal table in which each row is a top level being broken down to construct another new table. Its structure is very close to dimensional stacks. Input Mapped Classifier works like a wrapper that specifies the mismatches between test and training data by trying to build a relation between data used in training which the classifier has been constructed based on and the received test cases or instances. Additive Regression classifier improves the performance of classifiers that are based on regression. Each iteration done uses the residuals generated from previous iterations. It can overcome overfitting problem but it takes extra time. IBK stands for Instance-Bases Learning with parameter K. Its will-known name is K-nearest Neighborhood (KNN), while it is used in Weka software as IBK. It determines the number of nearest neighbors to be used in the instance classification process. In

2009, K-Star classifier was first introduced by Hussain Aljazzar. K means the number of shortest paths that can be found between a selected group of data points in a given graph.

Gussian Processes classifier can be considered as an example of non-parametric algorithms. It is used to deduce a distribution of random variables collection over functions. It attempts to find the similar points within the distribution to forecast the value. Linear regression is a ML algorithm that is classified under supervised learning. It predicts values based on the independently provided attributes. It is widely used in finding relationships between datasets attributes and prediction studies. So this classifier tries to find a linear relationship between the input values and the one to be predicted. Multi-Layer Perceptron is a neural network algorithm that consists of three main layers which are input layer, at least one hidden layer, then an output layer. Depending on the dataset and the problem, one or more nodes can compose the output layer.

Table 3: Datasets attributes description

Table-1. Datasets attributes description.

Item no.	Attribute	Description	Type
1	ID	Object ID	Positive integer
2	Effort	The actual total hours expended on the implementing process	Positive integer
3	IntComplx	The level of the internal calculation's complexity	1 to 5 that mean low to very high
4	DataEn	Total number of data-entry items	Positive number
5	DataFile	Total number of data-files accessed	Positive number
6	DataOut	Total number of data-output items	Positive number
7	UFP	Unadjusted function point count	Positive number
8	Lang	Language used	Language name
9	Tools	Used platforms and development tools	Tools/platform name
10	ToolExpr	Language and tool experience level	Range of number of months of experience
11	AppExpr	Applications experience level	1 to 5 which means low to very high
12	TeamSize	Size of the developing team	Range of min. to max. number
13	DBMS	Used DBMS	Database system name
14	Method	The used implementation methodology	e.g. OO, JAD
15	AppType	The used architecture	e.g. C/S, Centered
16	ObjType	Type of the object	PJ-project, FT- feature, RQ- requirement
17	Funct%	Percentage of functionality of features or requirements	1 to 7

Source: Dataset available at: http://tunedit.org/repo/PROMISE/EffortPrediction/usp05-ft.arff

The input signals spread forward within the network while error signals spread backward. To reduce the error, some weight adjustments are being made. SMOreg means Sequential Minimal Optimization that is an enhanced model of the SMO method which is based on support vector machine (SVM) used for regression. For un-linear prediction, SMOreg can be used in an efficient way. In SMOreg algorithm, some efficiency problems can be generated as a result of having one threshold.

3.2. Datasets and Evaluation Criteria

The datasets used in this work are prepared for software engineering experiments that are available publically. Two datasets will be used to test and compare the ML techniques, the first one is called usp05-ft and the second is usp05. The first one (Usp05-ft) contains 76 instances and consists of the first 15 attributes as described in Table 3.

3.2.1 Mean Absolute Error (MAE)

It is the absolute sum of the error divided by a number of predictions. The error is the difference between the actual effort and predicted effort.

3.2.2   Root Mean Squared Error (RMSE)

It is the square root of sum of the square error divided by the number of predictions. The error is the difference between the actual effort and predicted effort.

3.2.3   Relative Absolute Error (RAE)

It is the sum of the absolute error divided by sum of absolute relative error. The error is the difference between the actual effort and predicted effort, while the relative error is the difference between the actual effort and its mean.

3.2.4   Root Relative Squared Error (RRSE)

It is the square root of the square error divided by the square relative error. The error is the difference between the actual effort and predicted effort, while the relative error is the difference between the actual effort and its mean.

In addition to the 15 attributes, the second dataset (Usp05) contains 203 instances and consists of two more attributes which are 16 and 17 as described in Table 1. To evaluate the ML algorithms performance after applying them on the used datasets, five basic statistical indices were used as performance and assessment criteria. The indices are Mean Absolute Error, Root Mean Squared Error, Relative Absolute Error, and Root Relative.

3.2.5   Correlation Coefficient (R^2)

The correlation coefficient shows how the actual effort and predicted effort are related. It gives a value between -1 and 1. The correlation is 1 when the values increase together, and it goes down to -1 when there is no relation between the values. R^2 is computed as the following formula:
Squared Error, and Correlation Coefficient. Basically, they are measuring the error rate between the actual effort within the dataset and the predicted effort using the ML algorithm.
Assuming A is the actual effort, A is the predicted effort, A is the mean of A , and n is the number of instances, the following measures are used to evaluate the used ML models:

3.3 Data Mining

Weka tool version 3.8 has been used to evaluate the used algorithms. The 10 folds' cross-validation technique is used to train the data on 90% and test it on the remaining 10% until the whole data (100%) is being used as a test data through 10 cycles. Six types of classifiers have been used in Weka to test the 13 algorithms. The used classifiers or algorithms are Random Forest, REPTree, M5P, ZeroR, Decision Table, Input Mapped Classifier, Additive Regression, IBK, KStar, Gussian Processes, Linear Regression, Multilayer Perceptron, and SMOreg. The 13 methods have been tested on two datasets, the first one is (Usp05-ft) with 15 attributes and 76 instances. The second one (Usp05) is with 17 attributes and 203 instances.

Table 4 shows the results of applying the 13 algorithms on the dataset (Usp05-ft). The evaluation and comparison were done on 5 statistical error measures. The last row in Table 2 represents the average values for each measurement criteria.

Table 4: Performance results on dataset 1

Table-2. Performance results on usp05-ft dataset.

Method	R^2	MAE	RMSE	RAE %	RRSE %
Random forest	0.8441	2.5025	4.8546	41.7323	55.6778
REP tree	0.7607	3.2553	5.6754	54.2868	65.0918
M5P	0.705	3.2359	6.2428	53.9628	71.5994
ZeroR	-0.2644	5.9965	8.7191	100	100
Decision table	0.7137	3.4225	6.241	57.0738	71.579
Input- mapped- classifier	-0.2644	5.9965	8.7191	100	100
Additive- regression	0.7136	3.2441	6.5709	54.0993	75.363
IBK	0.7853	2.5132	5.8021	41.9101	66.5451
KStar	0.7797	2.7272	6.0219	45.4795	69.0658
Gussian- processes	0.7604	2.8814	5.6809	48.0511	65.1554
Linear- regression	-0.2644	5.9965	8.7191	100	100
Multilayer- perceptron	0.7979	2.8173	5.6413	46.9824	64.7004
SMOreg	0.7504	2.6597	6.2764	44.3547	71.9853
Average	0.5244	3.6345	6.5511	60.6102	75.1356

Table 5: Performance results on dataset 2

Table-3. Best and worst results on usp05-ft dataset.

Criteria	R^2	MAE	RMAE	RAE%	RRSE%
Best result Algorith m	0.8441 Random forest	2.5025 Random forest	4.8546 Random forest	41.7323 Random forest	55.6778 Random forest
Worst Result Algorith m	-0.2644 ZeroR, input mapped classifie r, and linear reg- ression	5.9965 ZeroR, input mapped classifie r, and linear reg- ression	8.7191 ZeroR, input mapped classifie r, and linear reg- ression	100 ZeroR, input mapped classifie r, and linear reg- ression	100 ZeroR, input mapped classifie r, and linear reg- ression
Average	0.28985	4.2495	6.78685	70.8662	77.8389

Table 3 shows the best and worst results scored among the 13 algorithms that have have been applied to the first dataset (Usp05-ft). In all types of statistical measurements used to test and evaluate the error rate, Random Forest scored the best results in all the indices with the lowest error rate for the four types (MAE, RMAE, RAE, RRSE) and highest correlation.

Table 4 represents the performance measurement results after applying the 13 algorithms on the second dataset (Usp05). Two more attributes have been added to the dataset and the number of instances is almost three times than the first dataset. The last row is showing the average value for each measurement criteria.

Table 6: Performance results on dataset 3

Table-4. Performance results on usp05 dataset.

Method	R^2	MAE	RMSE	RAE %	RRSE %
Random forest	0.4319	8.1464	31.8046	60.5244	92.3641
REP tree	0.6296	10.0367	29.757	74.569	86.4177
M5P	0.4628	9.9475	30.6858	73.9061	89.1151
ZeroR	-0.3113	13.4596	34.4339	100	100
Decision table	0.5118	8.7527	30.1391	65.0297	87.5273
Input- mapped- classifier	-0.3113	13.4596	34.4339	100	100
Additive- regression	0.558	8.445	28.2736	62.7431	82.1098
IBK	0.2504	8.7266	38.9912	64.8355	113.2349
KStar	0.3626	7.3318	32.1284	54.4729	93.3046
Gussian- processes	0.4978	8.2471	29.659	61.2729	86.1333
Linear- regression	-0.3113	13.4596	34.4339	100	100
Multilayer- perceptron	-0.022	15.7926	36.513	117.3334	106.038
SMOreg	0.4962	8.8851	29.5932	66.0134	85.9422
Average	0.2496	10.3608	32.3728	76.9770	94.0144

In this section, 13 ML algorithms have been evaluated using two datasets. The evaluation criteria used in this work are R^2, MAE, RMAE, RAE, and RRSE. The aim of the proposed model is to predict the effort using dataset attributes and compare them with the actual effort in order to measure the error using different criteria. The higher the value of R^2 the better result, for the rest of the measurement criteria, the lower value means a better result. Random Forest achieved the best results in the first experiment using (Usp05-ft) dataset and another three models which are REPTree, Additive Regression and Kstar scored the best results using (Usp05) dataset. ZeroR method scored the worst results using the first dataset while some other methods including Multilayer Perceptron, IBk, and Linear Regression didn't perform well on the second dataset.

In the future, more datasets can be included in the study to have a wider angle and more variety in the inputs which will be reflected to have a better estimation and more accurate results. Moreover, some other ML algorithms can be tested and involved in upcoming studies in order to cover all available machine learning methods.

4. COMPUTER NETWORKS AND COMMUNICATION SYSTEMS

The presence of any type of distortion in communication system, regardless of the causes, is undesirable and undeniably has a negative impacts on the system in general and therefore it is necessary to eliminate its effects. This study employs one of the well-known algorithms for adaptive equalization of linear dispersive communication channel which is Least Mean Square (LMS) algorithm. The LMS technique is basically utilized to eliminate the noise in communication channel. The novelty of this paper includes the profoundly analyzing of the influence of rate of convergence, miss-adjustment, computational requirement, and sensitivity to Eigen-value spread in sufficient details in a simple and plain way. Moreover, the system performance improvement employing the feedback equalizer technique is intensively presented which shows that our methodology is very effective to eliminate the noise in the system. The simulation work has been performed with MATLAB software.

Adaptive filters are used extensively in statistical signal processing and offer a great improvement in performance compared with the conventional fixed filters. The subject of adaptive filters in general and linear adaptive filters in particular has drawn the attention of many researchers and therefore a various methodologies have been developed and implemented to solve any given problem in the area of statistical signal processing. The linear adaptive filter includes a filter whose function is to produce a desired output, and an adaptive algorithm to set the filter parameters. The selected algorithm is significantly affected by the filter structure which is mainly classified into finite impulse filter (FIR) and infinite impulse response (IIR).

Generally, adaptive algorithm attempts to minimize the error function in the input, reference, and output signals to near zero value. The most commonly minimization methods used for adaptive filters are Quasi-Newton techniques and the steepest-descent gradient technique. The latter is easy to perform but the quasi-Newton strategy basically has better convergence rate. Therefore the best choice is the Quasi-Newton techniques which have better computational performance and good convergence. But disadvantage of this method is very sensitive to the instability matters. In all these strategies, it is necessary to select the convergence factor carefully based on the specific adaptation issue. The error signal normally is created in different ways but the most popular techniques are Mean Square Error (MSE) methodology, and Least Squares (LS) technique. MSE is requiring an infinite amount of data. The LS technique is consistent with the fixed data. Proper selection of the error signal basically impacts the selected algorithm complexity, and convergence rate.

Any adaptive application has to be carefully studied prior to selection of the adequate algorithm. The selection of algorithm must consider the computational cost, performance, and robustness. In this applied study we select the LMS algorithm rather than the other two well-known algorithms namely, Recursive Least Squres RLS and Recursive Least Squres Lattice RLSL algorithms that could be employed to solve problems related to the field of equalization. The main objective of using this strategy is to eliminate noise from the corrupted input signal and adapt the ATF weights in the way that the mean square of the estimated error is to be minimized. Upon applying the algorithm to the linear equalization we can study the various aspects, behaviours, advantages, and drawbacks of the technique. Moreover this technique, which is essentially employed in the field of adaptive filters, has many different applications in the fields of communications, computers and adaptive signal processing in general due to its computation simplicity.

4.1. Problem Formulation

It is necessary to eliminate the effects of distortion produced in the transmitting communication channel so as to produce the desired signal d(n) throughout the updating of the ATF weight. In this algorithm, which is the simplest one, we calculate the estimated error {e(n)=y(n) - d(n)}. This error is employed to update tap weight vector "w" values as follows:

Step 1: Select an initial weight vector, for example, w(0) = 0

Step 2: For each sample of the input sequence {u(n)}, n = 1,2,...,N, form the tap-input vector u(n), and compute the adaptive transversal ATF output y(n)= wT(n-1) u(n).

Step 3: Calculate the error e(n)=y(n)-d(n)

Step 4: Update w(n)=w(n-1)+ μ u(n) e(n)

Step 5: Go to Step 2 until n= N.

Figure 1 demonstrate the learning curves of two ATF sizes M=11, and M=21 for a channel with w=3.3 (corresponds to eigenvalue spread of 21.7132), SNR= 40dB, and μ=0.07. According to the second order analysis, the step-size parameter has to be less than (2/Mr(0)). The value of r(0) corresponds to w=3.3 is 1.2265 therefore μ shall be less than 0.148. We conclude that the value of μ =0.07 is appropriate to the ATF size M=11, and the averaged square error decreases with the increasing number of iterations and reaches steady state after iteration 300, but the case is different with adaptive transversal ATF order M=21, because the step size is so high so that the averaged square error is in ascending order. If we select proper step size μ, such as 0.035 and apply this for both ATF orders as shown in Figure 1, we come to know that the difference between both curves is insignificant. Therefore, based on this result we select the ATF order M=11. This selection is consistent with the fact that design of any system shall be cost effective, so it is not reasonable to select higher ATF order.

Figure 1: Mean Square Error (MSE) methodology

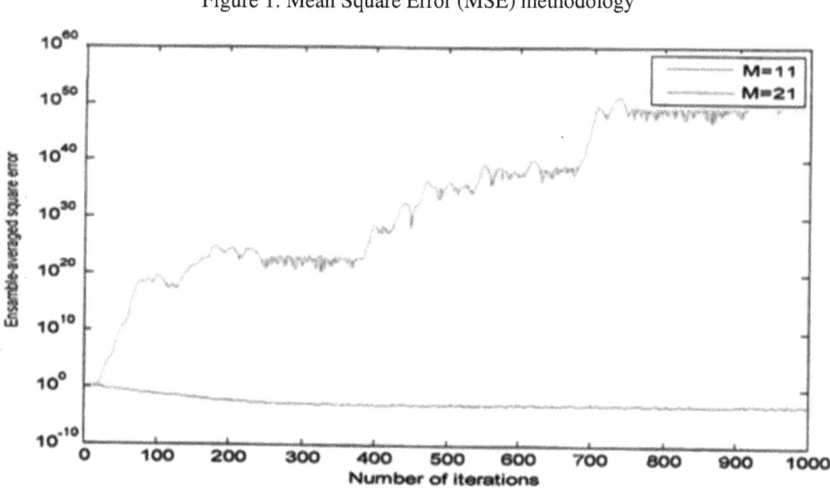

Figure 2: Convergence of LMS technique

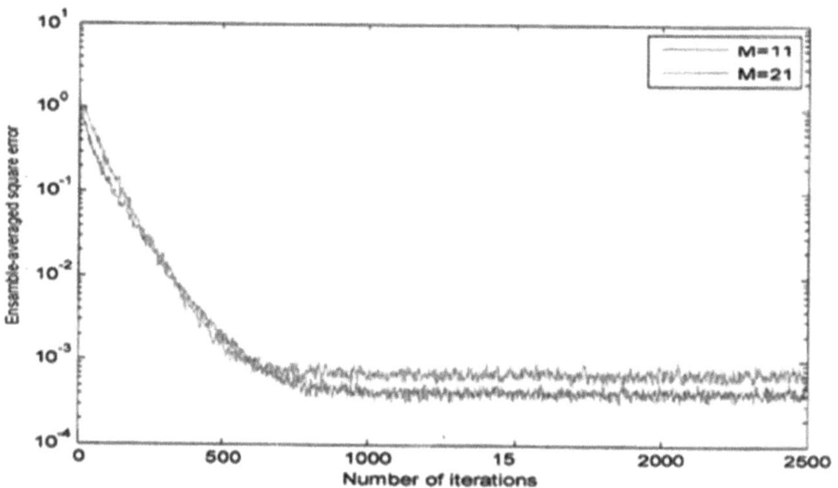

It is very necessary to compare this algorithm with others in the field of adaptive filter such as RLS algorithm in order to check the performance of this strategy in terms of their convergence rate of speed, sensitivity to channel distortion, the MSE, decision feedback equalizer and computational complexity. Here, we explain the prominent differences between both algorithms throughout their application on one problem.

4.2. Rate of Convergence

- LMS: This algorithm convergence speed is very sensitive to the eigenvalues spread variations. It is much slower than the RLS algorithm. As shown in Figure 1, the LMS technique converges to the steady state MSE after 160 iterations (for w =2.9) and after about 500 iterations for (w = 3.5).

- RLS: The speed of convergence of this strategy is relatively insensitive to the eigenvalue spreads variations. The RLS converges about 20 iterations.

4.3. Ensemble-Averaged Square Error

•   LMS: The averaged MSE in case of this algorithm is more sensitive than the RLS algorithm. As shown in

Figure 1, the range of variations in averaged MSE is from 0.004 for w = 3.5 to 0.0004 for w = 2.9.

•   RLS: The averaged MSE in this case is less sensitive to eigenvalues spread (w =2.9) and SNR of 40 dB.

4.4. Computational Complexity

•   LMS: This algorithm has the lowest computational complicity a among all algorithms in the field of adaptive filters.

•   RLS: This is much more complicated than LMS algorithm in computation complexity and implementation. More over LMS algorithm has a lower SNR compared with RLS technique.

We have profoundly discussed the results obtained using LMS algorithm in our study. It is clear that the strategy of cost-effective design of the system has been applied through the selection of the lower filter order (11) for the algorithm better performance. The impacts of eigenvalue spread and step–size parameter (μ) on LMS algorithm performance in terms of MSE reduction and convergence rate for different values of w and (μ) have been comprehensively analyzed. Moreover, the equalizer impulse response of different channels for eigenvalue spread and single channel with different (μ) for step-size parameter effect have been plotted and discussed. We conclude that the channels with lower w have a better performance in terms of both MSE and convergence for fixed step–size parameter (μ). On the other hand, the choice of step-size parameter (μ) for a fixed eigenvalue is a trade-off between convergence rate and misadjustment error and depends on the application that used for.

Unlike the other works performed in LMS technique, we have selected the decision feed-back equalizer (DFE) to improve the system efficiency and convergence rate. Comparison of learning curves of LMS algorithm of adaptive equalizer with and without feedback of fixed μ and same eigenvalue spread, shows higher convergence speed and better equalizer performance in case of employing feed-back filter so that the averaged MSE has been reduced more than 40 times with feed-back filter.Therfore, we recommend this decision feedback equalizer for other algorithms in the field of noise cancellation in communication channels.

5. FUTURE DIRECTION

Statistical detection methods are used to reduce the search space and it can be used for correlations between a pair of univariate time-series model, and among multiple univariate and multivariate time-series models. An approach to model, detect and analyze high level spatio-temporal events in public health surveillance can be proposed that would allow healthcare analysts to view high incidences of events in proper and broader context. Future directions extending the current work would lead us to more accurate detection by isolating frequency components from time series and extending the temporal patterns towards spatial domain.

Aggregate chief complaint count variable can be decomposed into derived frequency components by STL filtering based methods. Results from previous section show the application of STL to extract intra-annual seasonal and weekly components from aggregates time series. Future work would include extending the change point detection method to remainder component of time series when effect of periodicity and others have been removed. A comparison with current results would indicate whether this affects the sensitivity or any other parameter of detection. As a future work we can extend change-point detection techniques for multiple change points between various segments of time series. We can also look at other anomaly indicator functions such as; change in variance and transformation of data distribution itself.

BIBLIOGRAPHY

[1] C. E. Sharp and M. Rowe. "Online games and e-business: Architecture for integrating business models and services into online games", IBM Systems Journal, Volume 45, 2006.

[2] A. Spurling. "QoS issues for multiplayer gaming", July, 2004
http://users.cs.cf.ac.uk/O.F.Rana/data-comms/

[3] R. Joshi, "Data oriented Architecture: A loosely Coupled Real time SOA." Real-Time Innovations, Inc, CA, Tech. Rep. Aug 2007.

[4] Quake II. http://www.idsoftware.com/games/quake/quake2/

[5] A. Bharambe, J. Pang and S. Seshan, "Colyseus: a distributed architecture for online multiplayer games", In Proceedings of the 3rd conference on Networked Systems Design & Implementation, pp.12-12, May 08-10, 2006, San Jose, CA

[6] Cronin E., Kurc A. R., Filstrup B., Jamin S., "An Efficient. Synchronization Mechanism for Mirrored Game Architectures", In Proceedings of ACM netgames, April 2002.

[7] A. R. Bharambe, J. R. Douceur, J. R. Lorch, T. Moscibroda, J. Pang, S. Seshan, X. Zhuang, "Donnybrook: enabling large-scale, high-speed, peer-to-peer games", SIGCOMM 2008: pp 389-400.

[8] KNUTSSON, B. ET AL. "Peer-to-peer support for massively multiplayer games". In Proceedings of the INFOCOM, July 2004.

[9] H. Jin, H. Yao, X. Liao, S. Yang, W. Liu and Y. Jia, "PKTown: A Peer-to-Peer Middleware to Support Multiplayer Online Games", Multimedia and Ubiquitous Engineering, 2007. MUE '07, International Conference on, April 2007.

[10] M. Assiotis and V. Tzanov, "A distributed architecture for MMORPG", Proceedings of 5th ACM SIGCOMM workshop on network and system support for games, 2006.

[11] C. G. Dickey, D. Zappala, V. Lo, "Distributed architecture for Massively-Multiplayer Online Games", ACM NetGames Workshop, August, 2004.

[12] A. Bharambe, J. Pang, S. Seshan, "Colyseus: a distributed architecture for online multiplayer games", Proceedings of the 3rd conference on Networked Systems Design & Implementation, 2006.

[13] B. D. Vleeschauwer, B. V. D. Bossche, T. Verdickt, F. D. Turck, B. Dhoedt, and P. Demeester. "Dynamic microcell assignment for massively multiplayer online gaming", In

NetGames '05: Proceedings of 4th ACM SIGCOMM workshop on Network and system support for games, pages 1–7, New York, NY, USA, 2005. ACM.

[14] M. Assiotis and V. Tzanov, "A distributed architecture for MMORPG", Proceedings of 5th ACM SIGCOMM workshop on Network and system support for games, 2006.

[15] D. Zindel, "Postina: A Publish/Subscribe Middleware Designed for Massively Multiplayer Games", April 2008, http://postina.zindel.org

[16] M. Bell, "Introduction to Service-Oriented Modeling". Service-Oriented Modeling: Service Analysis, Design, and Architecture. Wiley & Sons. pp. 3, 2008.

[17] J. Pasley, "How BPEL and SOA are changing web services development," IEEE Internet computing, Jun 2005.

[18] Data Distribution Service for Real Time Systems, Version 1.2, OMG specifications. http://www.omg.org/cgi-bin/doc?dds/06-04-05

[19] Mehdi Bahrami, Mohammad Bahrami "An overview to Software Architecture in Intrusion Detection System", International Journal of Soft Computing and Software Engineering [JSCSE], Vol. 1, No. 1, pp. 1-8, 2011.

[20] Yongbo Jiang, Zhiliang Qiu, Jian Zhang, Jun Li "Integration of Unicast and Multicast Scheduling in Input-Queued Packet Switches with High Scalability", International Journal of Soft Computing and Software Engineering [JSCSE], Vol. 2, No. 4, pp. 14-34, 2012.

[21] Zaigham Mahmood, "The Promise and Limitations of Service Oriented Architecture", International Journal of Computers, Vol. 1, No. 3, pp. 74-78, 2007.

[22] Alexandre Denault, Jörg Kienzle, "Journey: A Massively Multiplayer Online Game Middleware," IEEE Software, vol. 28, no. 5, pp. 38-44, Sept.-Oct. 2011.

[23] Ginhung Wang, Kuochen Wang, "An efficient hybrid P2P MMOG cloud architecture for dynamic load management," pp.199-204, The International Conference on Information Network 2012.

[24] Farrukh Arslan, "Towards Service Oriented Architecture (SOA) for Massive Multiplayer Online Games (MMOG)," pp.538-543, 2012 UKSim 14th International Conference on Computer Modelling and Simulation, 2012.

[25] S. Kumari and S. Pushkar, "Cuckoo search based hybrid models for improving the accuracy of software effort estimation," *Microsystem Technologies,* vol. 24, pp. 4767-4774, 2018. Available at: https://doi.org/10.1007/s00542-018-3871-9.

[26] P. Pospieszny, B. Czarnacka-Chrobot, and A. Kobylinski, "An effective approach for software project effort and duration estimation with machine learning algorithms," *The Journal of Systems & Software,* vol. 137, pp. 184–196, 2018. Available at: https://doi.org/10.1016/j.jss.2017.11.066.

[27] K. Langsari, R. Sarno, and Sholiq, "Optimizing effort parameter of COCOMO II using particle swarm optimization method," *Telkomnika,* vol. 16, pp. 2208-2216, 2018. Available at: https://doi.org/10.12928/telkomnika.v16i5.9703.

[28] I. Attarzadeh and S. H. Ow, "Improving estimation accuracy of the COCOMO II using an adaptive fuzzy logic model," presented at the 2011 IEEE International Conference on Fuzzy Systems, Taipei, Taiwan, 2011.

[29] R. Litoriya, N. Sharma, and D. A. Kothari, "Incorporating cost driver substitution to improve the effort using Agile COCOMO II," presented at the 2012 CSI Sixth International Conference on Software Engineering, 2012.

[30] R. Saljoughinejad and V. Khatibi, "A new optimized hybrid model based On COCOMO to increase the accuracy of software cost estimation," *Journal of Advances in Computer Engineering and Technology,* vol. 4, pp. 27-40, 2018.

[31] Z. Chen, T. Menzies, D. Port, and B. Boehm, "Feature subset selection can improve software cost estimation accuracy," *ACM SIGSOFT Software Engineering Notes,* vol. 30, pp. 1-6, 2005. Available at: https://doi.org/10.1145/1082983.1083171.

[32] Z. A. Khalifelu and F. S. Gharehchopogh, "Comparison and evaluation of data mining techniques with algorithmic models in software cost estimation," *Procedia Technology,* vol. 1, pp. 65-71, 2012. Available at: https://doi.org/10.1016/j.protcy.2012.02.013.

[33] P. A. Whigham, C. A. Owen, and S. G. Macdonell, "A baseline model for software effort estimation," *ACM Transactions on Software Engineering and Methodology,* vol. 24, pp. 1-11, 2015. Available at: https://doi.org/10.1145/2738037.

[34] F. Sarro, A. Petrozziello, and M. Harman, "Multi-objective software effort estimation," presented at the ACM 38th IEEE International Conference on Software Engineering, 2016.

[35] Y. Masoudi-Sobhanzadeh, H. Motieghader, and A. Masoudi-Nejad, "Feature select: A software for feature selection based on machine learning approaches," *BMC Bioinformatics,* vol. 20, pp. 1-17, 2019. Available at: https://doi.org/10.1186/s12859-019-2754-0.

[36] V. Vig and A. Kaur, "Test effort estimation and prediction of traditional and rapid release models using machine learning algorithms," *Journal of Intelligent & Fuzzy Systems,* vol. 35, pp. 1657-1669, 2018. Available at: https://doi.org/10.3233/jifs-169703.

[37] A. Khalid, M. A. Latif, and M. Adnan, "An approach to estimate the duration of software project through machine learning techniques," *Gomal University Journal of Research,* vol. 33, pp. 1-13, 2017.

[38] T.-H. Yeh and S. Deng, "Application of machine learning methods to cost estimation of product life cycle," *International Journal of Computer Integrated Manufacturing,* vol. 25, pp. 340-352, 2012. Available at: https://doi.org/10.1080/0951192x.2011.645381.

[39] M. D. Ganggayah, N. A. Taib, Y. C. Har, P. Lio, and S. K. Dhillon, "Predicting factors for survival of breast cancer patients using machine learning techniques," *BMC Medical Informatics and Decision Making,* vol. 19, pp. 1-17, 2019. Available at: https://doi.org/10.1186/s12911-019-0801-4.

[40] P. Pandey, "Analysis of the techniques for software cost estimation," presented at the 2013 Third International Conference on Advanced Computing and Communication Technologies (ACCT), Rohtak, India, 2013.

[41] B. Başkeleş, B. Turhan, and A. Bener, "Software effort estimation using machine learning methods," presented at the 2007 22nd International Symposium on Computer & Information Sciences, 2007.

[42] J. Rahikkala, S. Hyrynsalmi, V. Leppänen, and I. Porres, "The role of organisational phenomena in software cost estimation: A case study of supporting and hindering factors," *E-Informatica Software Engineering Journal,* vol. 12, pp. 167–198, 2018.

[43] M. Vyas, A. Bohra, D. C. Lamba, and A. Vyas, "A review on software cost and effort estimation techniques for agile development process," *International Journal of Recent Research Aspects,* vol. 5, pp. 612-618, 2016.

[44] S. A. Woznicki, J. Baynes, S. Panlasigui, M. Mehaffey, and A. Neale, "Development of a spatially complete floodplain map of the conterminous United States using random forest," *Science of the Total Environment,* vol. 647, pp. 942-953, 2019. Available at: https://doi.org/10.1016/j.scitotenv.2018.07.353.

[45] S. Kalmegh, "Analysis of weka data mining algorithm reptree, simple cart and randomtree for classification of Indian news," *International Journal of Innovative Science, Engineering & Technology,* vol. 2, pp. 438-446, 2015.

[46] S.-A. Blaifi, S. Moulahoum, R. Benkercha, B. Taghezouit, and A. Saim, "M5P model tree based fast fuzzy maximum power point tracker," *Solar Energy,* vol. 163, pp. 405-424, 2018. Available at: https://doi.org/10.1016/j.solener.2018.01.071.

[47] T. Rajasekaran, P. Jayasheelan, and K. S. Preethaa, "Predictive analysis in agriculture to improve the crop productivity using zeroR algorithm," *International Journal of Computer Science and Engineering Communications,* vol. 4, pp. 1397-1401, 2016.

[48] B. G. Becker, "Visualizing decision table classifiers," in *Proceedings IEEE Symposium on Information Visualization*, 1998.

[49] Class Input Mapped Classifier, Available: http://weka.sourceforge.net, 2019.

[50] Additive Regression, Available: https://www.cs.waikato.ac.nz/ml/weka/, 2019.

[51] Gerardnico, "Machine learning - K-nearest neighbors (KNN) algorithm - instance based learning." Available: https://gerardnico.com/, 2017.

[52] University of Konstanz, "K* Algorithm (K Star)." Available: https://www.sen.uni-konstanz.de/, 2019.

[53] M. Krasser, "Gaussian processes." Available: http://krasserm.github.io, 2018.

[54] Geeksforgeeks, "ML linear regression." Available: https://www.geeksforgeeks.org, 2019.

[55] P. Singh and S. Agrawal, "Node localization in wireless sensor networks using the M5P tree and SMOreg algorithms," presented at the 2013 5th International Conference and Computational Intelligence and Communication Networks. IEEE, 2013.

[56] M. Vrankic, D. Sersic, and V. Sucic, "Adaptive 2-D wavelet transform based on the lifting scheme with preserved vanishing moments," *IEEE Transactions on Image Processing,* vol. 19, pp. 1987-2004, 2010. Available at: https://doi.org/10.1109/tip.2010.2045688.

[57] P. Sathawane and D. Prasanthi, "An optimal low power adaptive filter design for noise reduction," *International Journal of Science, Engineering and Technology Research,* vol. 3, pp. 2405-2410, 2014.

[58] S.-W. Sohn, Y.-B. Lim, J.-J. Yun, H. Choi, and H.-D. Bae, "A filter bank and a self-tuning adaptive filter for the harmonic and interharmonic estimation in power signals," *IEEE*

Transactions on Instrumentation and Measurement, vol. 61, pp. 64-73, 2011. Available at: https://doi.org/10.1109/tim.2011.2150610.

[59] L. Stankovic, "Performance analysis of the adaptive algorithm for bias-to-variance tradeoff," *IEEE Transactions on Signal Processing,* vol. 52, pp. 1228-1234, 2004. Available at: https://doi.org/10.1109/tsp.2004.826179.

[60] J. Cerqueira and S. Haddad, "Design of a low power adaptive LMS equalizer for hearing-aid applications," in *2014 IEEE Biomedical Circuits and Systems Conference (Bio CHS) Proceedings. Lausanne, Switzerland, Oct. 22-24, 2014.*

[61] Y. Ahmed and A. Hoballah, "Adaptive filter-FLC integration for torque ripples minimization in PMSM using PSO," *International Journal of Power Electronics and Drive Systems,* vol. 10, pp. 48-57, 2019. Available at: https://doi.org/10.11591/ijpeds.v10.i1.pp48-57.

[62] M. S. Salman, A. Eleyan, and B. Al-Sheikh, "Discrete wavelet transform-based RI adaptive algorithm for system identification," *International Journal of Electrical and Computer Engineering,* vol. 10, pp. 2383-2391, 2020. Available at: https://doi.org/10.11591/ijece.v10i3.pp2383-2391.

[63] G. Samanta and A. Chandra, "A novel design strategy of low-pass FIR filter using opposition- based differential evolution algorithm," in *2012 IEEE Students Conference on Electrical, Electronic and Computer Science (SCEECS), Bhopal, India, Mar. 1-2,* 2012, pp. 1-4.

[64] T. Moon, "Universal switching FIR filtering," *IEEE Transactions on Signal Processing,* vol. 60, pp. 1460-1464, 2011. Available at: https://doi.org/10.1109/tsp.2011.2176931.

[65] K. e. a. Rana, "Efficient FIR filter designs using constrained genetic algorithms based optimization," in *2016 2nd international Conference on Communication Control and Intelligent Systems (CCIS), Muthaura, India, Nov.18-20, 2016.*

[66] S. K. Saha, S. P. Ghoshal, R. Kar, and D. Mandal, "Cat swarm optimization algorithm for optimal linear phase FIR filter design," *ISA Transactions,* vol. 52, pp. 781-794, 2013. Available at: https://doi.org/10.1016/j.isatra.2013.07.009.

[67] M. Sababha and M. Zohdy, "Linear phase FIR low pass filter design based on firefly algorithm," *International Journal of Electrical and Computer Engineering (IJECE),* vol. 8, pp. 4356-4365, 2018. Available at: https://doi.org/10.11591/ijece.v8i6.pp4356-4365.

[68] M. Rajmohan and H. Shekhar, "Design of parallel and pipelined DA based OBC FIR filter for software defined radio," *Indonesian Journal of Electrical Engineering and Computer*

Science, vol. 14, pp. 1228-1234, 2019. Available at: https://doi.org/10.11591/ijeecs.v14.i3.pp1228-1234.

[69] H. Chen, S. Chan, and K. Ho, "A semi-definite programming (SDP) method for designing," *Proceedings, Vancouver,* vol. 3, pp. 149-152, 2004.

[70] S. C. e. a. Chan, "A new method for designing FIR/IIR digital correction filters for time-interleaved analog-to-digital converter using second order cone programming," in *IEEE 50th Midwest Symposium on Circuits and Systems, Montreal, Que, Canada,* 2007, pp. 1030 – 1033.

[71] P. Dighe and M. Chinchamalatpure, "High speed multiplier as IIR filter design using vedic mathematics," *International Journal for technological research in engineering,* vol. 4, pp. 1198-2201, 2017.

[72] Q. Liu, Y. C. Lim, and Z. Lin, "Design of pipelined IIR filters using two-stage frequency-response masking technique," *IEEE Transactions on Circuits and Systems II: Express Briefs,* vol. 66, pp. 873-877, 2019.

[73] E. e. a. Asmae, "Meta-heuristic techniques for optimal design of analog and digital filter," *Indonesian Journal of Electrical Engineering and Computer Science,* vol. 19, p. 669~679, 2020.

[74] A. Fominyh, "Application of the steepest descent method to solving differential Inclusions with either free or fixed right end," in *2017 IEEE Conference on Constructive Non Smooth Analysis and Related Topics (CNSA), St. Petersburg, Russia, May 22-27,* 2017, pp. 1-4.

[75] M. Z. A. Bhotto and A. Antoniou, "Robust quasi-Newton adaptive filtering algorithms," *IEEE Transactions on Circuits and Systems II: Express Briefs,* vol. 58, pp. 537-541, 2011.

[76] Y. Dong and H. Zhao, "A new proportionate normalized least mean square algorithm for high measurement noise," in *2015 IEEE International Conference on Signal Processing, Communications and Computing (ICSPCC), Ningbo, China, Sep. 19-22,* 2015, pp. 1-5.

[77] S. M. H. Irid, M. H. Hachemi, E. A. Haroun, and M. Hadjila, "Spectrum sensing with VSS-NLMS process in femto/macro-cell environments," *International Journal of Electrical and Computer Engineering,* vol. 8, pp. 5185-5205, 2018. Available at: https://doi.org/10.11591/ijece.v8i6.pp5185-5194.

[78] P. e. a. Zhu, "A new variable step size LMS algorithm for a pplication to underwater acoustic channel equalization," in *2017 IEEE International Conference on Signal Processing, Communication and Computing (ICSPCC), Xiamen, China, Oct. 22-25, 2017,* pp. 1- 4.

[79] A. e. a. Mohammad, "Improvement of LMS adaptive noise canceller using uniform Polyphase digital filter bank," *Indonesian Journal of Electrical Engineering and Computer Science,* vol. 17, pp. 1258-1265, 2020.

[80] Y. e. a. WE, "Adaptive notch filter based on LMS algorithm and its application in ground tilt data processing," in *2012 2nd IEEE International Conference on Consumer Electronics, Communications and Networks (CECNet), Yichang, China, Apr. 21-23,* 2012, pp. 2345 – 2348.

[81] C. M. Rao, D. B. S. Charles, M. G. Prasad, and S. Principal, "A variation of LMS algorithm for noise cancellation," *International Journal of Advanced Research in Computer and Communication Engineering,* vol. 2, pp. 2838-2843, 2013.

[82] S. Prasad and S. Patil, "Implementation of LMS algorithm for system identification," in *2016 IEEE International Conference on Signal and Information Processing (IConSIP), Vishnupuri, India,* 2016, pp. 1-5.

[83] N. Krishnamoorthy, I. Rajkumar, J. Alexander, and D. Marshiana, "Performance analysis of bio-signal processing in ocean environment using soft computing techniques," *International Journal of Electrical and Computer Engineering,* vol. 10, p. 2944, 2020.

[84] S. M. Jung, J.-H. Seo, and P. Park, "Variable step-size non-negative normalised least-mean-square-type algorithm," *IET Signal Processing,* vol. 9, pp. 618-622, 2015.

[85] H. e. a. Li, "A new LMS algorithm with application to fixed Satellite communications," in *IEEE 3rd International Workshop on Advanced Computational Intelligence (IWACI), Suzhou, China, Aug. 25-27,* 2010, pp. 72-75.

[86] R. e. a. Ramli, "Objective and subjective evaluations of adaptive noise cancellation systems with selectable algorithms for speech intelligibility," *Bulletin of Electrical Engineering and Informatics,* vol. 7, pp. 570-579, 2018.

[87] M. e. a. Rahman, "Development of decision feedback equalizer using simplified adaptive algorithms," *Journal of Critical Reviews,* vol. 7, pp. 305-309, 2020.

[88] H. Bierk and M. Alsaedi, "Recursive least squares algorithm for adaptive transversal equalization of linear dispersive communication channel," *Journal of Engineering Science and Technology, School of Engineering, Taylor University,* vol. 14, pp. 1043-1054, 2019.

[89] S. e. a. Patel, "Comparative study of LMS & RLS algorithms for adaptive filter design with FPGA," *Progress in Science in Engineering Research Journal,* vol. 2, pp. 185-192, 2014.

Printed by Books on Demand GmbH, Norderstedt / Germany